THE WEEPING DESTINY

Answering the Cry of Purpose in a Noisy World

AYO OLUFEMI

For question, feedback, or enquiries about this book you can reach out to the author;

Email: *dailyaffirmations80@gmail.com*
Tel. : +13174289361
IG: femianiyi

ISBN: 978-1-0090-4358-8

Published by:

Emphaloz Publishing House
publish@emphaloz.com)

Globally Available

Dedication

To my dearest aunt and best friend, Esther Olufemi, who slept in the Lord in 2007, I still miss you every day. Your love, wisdom, and warmth remain etched in my heart. This book is also for every soul who stood by me in moments of hardship. Your faith in me reignited the courage to believe in my purpose and keep pressing forward. Thank you for being my inspiration.

Acknowledgments

First and foremost, I give all glory to God — the source of my strength, wisdom, and purpose. Without His grace, none of this would have been possible.

To my loving wife, your devotion, encouragement, and unshakable belief in my dreams have been my constant fuel. Thank you for standing by me through the darkest seasons and celebrating every small victory.

To my beautiful children, your laughter and presence remind me daily of why I must keep pushing forward. You are my greatest treasures.

A big thanks to my pastor and every member of the Redeemed Christian Church of God, Kings Court, Fairfield, Ohio, for accepting us and welcoming us into the big family. We deeply appreciate all the love. A very special thank you to my fathers in the Lord — Pastor Tony Fasoore of RCCG Covenant House Indianapolis, Pastor K. Balogun of RCCG Rod of God, Indianapolis, and Pastor Daves Oludare Fasipe, General Overseer of Everlasting Hope International

Ministries, Indianapolis. Your spiritual guidance, prayers, and unwavering support have been instrumental in my journey.

To my uncles — Emmanuel Odunayo Olufemi, Clement Olufemi, Blessing Olufemi, and Pastor David Oluwaseun — thank you for your unwavering support and presence during my formative years. Your guidance and encouragement have been pillars in my journey.

To every reader holding this book: thank you. May this journey ignite something powerful in you. May your destiny rise from the ashes and find its voice through these words.

...in Their Words

Ayo Olufemi is a visionary leader known for standing firmly behind everything he believes in, his presence is both inspiring and empowering. His unwavering support uplifts every project he touches, and his deep love for his family and those around him reflects the heart of a man rooted in purpose.

He leads with conviction, lives with intention, and leaves a lasting impact wherever he goes.

Olubayo Ajayi (@Bay2Joe)

Ayo Niyi Olufemi writes with a rare depth, pouring raw emotion, vivid thought, and powerful narrative into every page. His stories are not just told — they are felt, lived, and remembered. Driven by an unwavering love for his children and family, his words carry a warmth that reflects his heart. Beyond storytelling, Ayo's passion for uplifting others shines through, making his work both moving and meaningful.

Akintayo Akinola (Tayo Knights)

Bro Niyi, as I fondly call him, is a brilliant and passionate individual who has always been driven by a thirst for knowledge, exploring many paths yet with one unshakable focus: humanity. His unwavering commitment to both his profession and to bettering the lives of others is truly inspiring. I have no doubt that this book is a reflection of his incredible focus, intelligence, multitasking and meticulous nature.

Dr. Falebita Oluwanife

Ayo Olufemi is a truly brilliant writer whose exceptional talent shines through every page of his work. As the editor and project manager of his first book, Concealed, I was captivated by his unique and insightful perspectives. Beyond his literary prowess, Ayo possesses a truly great personality, making him a joy to collaborate with and an author everyone who has crossed paths with him is genuinely proud of. He is indeed a "sui generis" and a very deserving champion.

Oluseyi Ogunlana (Don Fiesta)
Media Practitioner & Publisher, Fiesta
International Magazine

Mr. Ayo Olufemi is a brilliant, analytical, and spirit-filled individual whose selflessness and generosity have left a lasting impact on many. Over 24 years ago, he became the pioneer Editor-in-Chief of the Redeemed Christian Fellowship, College of Education, Ikere-Ekiti Chapter, successfully producing the maiden edition of the fellowship's JET Magazine. Even in his early years, his heart of gold was evident—famously giving up his bed space to accommodate new students (myself included) and sharing his food even when it meant going without. Having known him for 23 years, I can confidently say that his unwavering kindness, deep introspection, and commitment to uplifting others have made him a beloved and respected figure in every community he's part of.

Tolulope Adeniran
(Former RCF President, COE, Ikere-Ekiti)

The values espoused in this book by Ayo Olufemi cannot be disconnected from the virtues that the author exhibits. The author is a humble, honest, trustworthy and compassionate family man. His hospitality knows no bounds. I recalled a treat to a sumptuous meal of pounded yam during one of my visits to the U.S. To this day, the memory of the meal lingers on. I therefore commend the author for this great publication, and hope that he continues to use his creativity to transform society.

Otunba Bamidele Ologunloluwa
(Former Commissioner, Ondo State)

I've known Mr. Ayodeji Olufemi since 2015, and right from the start, I knew he was someone truly special. I often refer to him as a "special child" — not just because of his brilliance, but because he carries a depth of wisdom far beyond his years. He's not only gifted in finance, but he's also kind, humble, and deeply rooted in character. A father, a friend, and a man who brings peace with him wherever he goes. There's one moment I'll never forget. He looked at me and said, *"Dunni, you're very intelligent and smart — don't let anyone dim your light."* That's Ayodeji in a sentence. He sees the light in people and speaks directly to it. He's warm, wise, and always cheerful — a rare blend of discipline and joy, whether in his actions or his words.

Akinwumi Oladunni Hellen (@holadunnni)

The book, "The Weeping Destiny" written by Ayo Olaniyi, is a masterpiece full of personal experiences and reminiscences of life. It is a record of relationships in a typical family that requires the wisdom and guidance of God to navigate. Olaniyi has provided practical steps to address misunderstandings and misgivings in family settings. He highlighted the basic tools for harmony and peace in our homes as none is immune to crisis and challenges. I therefore have no doubt to recommend this book to all for refreshments, peace, and joy in our families, which primarily rests on 'letting go' of our pains.

Rev'd. 'Somo Ogunlade

Uncle Femi, as I fondly call him, is one of those authors who are deeply passionate about the artistic expression of real-life experiences. The world needs more writers and authors like him, because I believe the world needs more nonfiction stories than fiction.

@abiola_a_ somkitchen.ng

For Olufemi Ayo Olaniyi, a.k.a SETO, writing is an extension of his lifelong mission; helping those in need. As an author, he channels his deep empathy and experience into stories and insights designed to inspire change, offer support, and illuminate paths forward.

Jonathan O. Ayilaran *(Technical Expert Nigerian Senate Committee on Ethics Code of Conduct and Public Petitions.)*

Mr. Ayo Olufemi has always been a kind, supportive, and dependable presence, someone whose honesty and straightforward nature is both rare and refreshing. Your words carry weight because they come from a place of truth and integrity. You make people feel seen, heard, and encouraged just by being yourself. It's an honor to celebrate with you and witness this exciting milestone in your journey.

Mrs. Damilola Faneti (RN)

Ayo Olufemi has learned to rise through adversity, turning trials into testimonies.

In this timely book, he offers more than stories; he offers a pathway to peace.

At its core is a powerful truth: forgiveness is not weakness.

It is healing.

This is more than a book. It is a release.

Damilare Oluwasegun (Asiricomedy)
Author, International MC and Mediapreneur

Ayo Olufemi is a passionate writer and speaker whose work calls people to awaken to purpose and healing. Drawing from personal experiences of rejection and forgiveness, he inspires others to overcome pain and embrace destiny. His writing is marked by deep reflection, spiritual insight, and a conviction that no life event is accidental.

Oluseyi Akigbogun
CEO Allsocks Limited

Baba Seto, as I fondly call him, has been a good brother and friend over the past three years. In that time, I've come to know him as a truly humble, respectful, and honest family man. He's always ready to offer sincere advice and share helpful information — consistently uplifting those around him to do better.

Oluwasina Oyesanmi (A.K.A. Spero)

Some chase greatness with grand gestures; others build it quietly, with intention and grace. The most remarkable individuals aren't always in the spotlight — they're the ones whose steady resolve, sharp intellect, and enduring resilience shape the world around them. This is a tribute to one such person.

Olaniyi's unwavering dedication continues to inspire. As an executive member of the Itaogbolu Progressive Youth Movement in the early 2000s, 'Niyi brought boundless creativity and vibrant energy to his service. It's no surprise to witness the strides he's made decades later. I'm deeply proud of him.

Victor Ogunmola (D.O.) President of the American Association of Petroleum Geologists, African Region

Foreword

There are moments in a pastor's life when God allows you to witness not just a testimony, but the birthing of healing through brokenness. This book is one of those moments. When the author and his wife came into my office to share the progress of this book, I had no idea our conversation would turn into a divine encounter. What began as a discussion about writing soon opened into a deep well of pain — wounds carried for years, battles fought in silence, and scars that still bled beneath the surface. As I listened, my heart broke — not just because of the suffering, but because I recognized something many never talk about: the weight of betrayal from those closest to us. But what moved me even more was not the pain but the posture. The author wasn't seeking revenge or pity. He was seeking release and wholeness. This book is not based on theory; it is born from experience. Every line drip with the honesty of someone who has walked through rejection, loved through pain, and chosen forgiveness over bitterness. It takes incredible courage to relive such stories. It takes even greater grace to release those who wounded you. And it takes the Spirit of God to turn that pain into purpose. In the pages that follow, you will not only read a testimony – you will be invited into your own healing journey. Whether you've been hurt by family, abandoned by loved ones, or struggle to forgive yourself, this book will meet you at the crossroads of pain and destiny. Like Joseph in Egypt, the message here is clear: You can forgive and fulfill your calling. As the author's pastor and a witness to his spiritual journey, I can confidently say this message is for you. God is calling you to heal – not just for your peace, but for your purpose. Don't allow unforgiveness to become the silent thief of your destiny. Let this book lead you into the freedom that only Christ can give. To everyone who opens these pages: read slowly. Reflect deeply. Let go fully. And above all, embrace the freedom and peace that forgiveness brings.

You are not alone. You are not forgotten. And you are not beyond healing.

With love and conviction,
Pastor Michael Olaniyan
RCCG – King's Court Parish Fairfield, Ohio, USA

Table of Contents

Introduction

Nothing has ever happened to you by chance. Life's circumstances are not accidental; they are interconnected events shaping your path. *The Weeping Destiny* is not just a book—it is a call to awaken the sleeping giant in you. It is your manual to transformation, guiding you toward the best version of your life.

I've seen men anointed... but aimless. Gifted... but drifting. The weeping destiny isn't about unbelievers—it's about those of us who walk with God, yet sleepwalk past our purpose. Like Samson, like Eli, like Jonah... Until destiny weeps, heaven will wait.

Unforgiveness can destroy destiny. It blinds the eyes and hardens the heart, making it difficult to recognize the mercy and grace of God that is active in our lives. It traps us in cycles of bitterness, blocking the healing and breakthrough we so desperately need.

While compiling this book, I went to see my pastor to discuss the project. During our conversation, I felt led to share some personal hurt — wounds I've carried for many years. I opened up about the pain I've endured from my mother and siblings since I was thirteen. Despite showing them love, compassion, grace, and even extending help in their times of need, I have often been met with hatred, rejection, slander, and even death wishes. It's been one of the toughest battles of my life. After all, how does one reconcile with the thought that a mother could withhold love from her own child — her first child?

In all this, I have seen the grace of God, and I have been blessed beyond measure with the unwavering love of my wife and children. They have been my fuel, my anchor, and my redemption. Their love has kept me standing when I had every reason to collapse under the weight of grief.

After listening quietly, my pastor leaned back in his chair, visibly emotional. Then he spoke words that pierced my soul. "Beyond being a pastor," he said, "I also operate in the prophetic. Let me ask you — do you know what Joseph did after he left prison and became the prime minister of Egypt?"

He continued, "Joseph had every reason and every opportunity to seek revenge. He could have denied his brothers food, sending them back to die in famine. He could have had Potiphar's wife arrested and imprisoned. But he did none of that. When Joseph saw his brothers — who no longer recognized him — he stepped aside and wept. He remembered the pain, the betrayal, the trauma. But in that moment, he let go. He released them — not because he harbored hatred, but because he chose wholeness over bitterness. He forgave Potiphar's wife. He forgave his brothers. He forgave everyone who had hurt him. And by doing that, he stayed connected to the divine purpose of God for his life."

By now, my eyes were filled with tears. My pastor looked me in the eye and said with certainty, "You must forgive them. I know you've forgiven before and they've hurt you again. But this time, don't just forgive — release them. Let go of the pain. Let go of the expectation of change. Forgive them, but create healthy distance if needed. Continue to love, continue to help, but free your heart from the prison of pain."

So many of us are limited in life, not because we lack talent, intelligence, or opportunities, but because we carry a shattered soul. We walk around daily with emotional wounds that bind us. Our destiny weeps — not because it's denied — but because we are slowly dying inside when we should be flourishing. Destiny cries out for healing. It longs for us to surrender our brokenness to God, so He can take the wheel and restore us.

Only when we forgive ourselves, and those who have wounded us, can we truly hear the cry of destiny — and respond.

So today, with a humble heart and the peace of God as my witness, I release everyone who has caused me pain — those who rejected, betrayed, slandered, and even wished me death. I forgive you. I let you go. I choose not to carry bitterness. I choose peace. I choose love. And to anyone I may have offended, knowingly or unknowingly, I sincerely ask for your forgiveness.

I am no longer bound. I am free. And I allow the peace of God to reign in every corner of my heart.

Let your life be a testimony, not a tragedy.

"It is when the inner man becomes alert to the call of heaven that you realize that your existence is not a product of chance, but of intention. This awareness births clarity and conviction."

Chapter One
The Awakening

There is an invisible, irresistible force pulling you toward your purpose. It is called *destiny*. While some respond to this call, many ignore it, distracted by noise, fear, or comfort zones.

In 2006, a friend came to me with an unusual proposal. He wanted us to visit a ritualist to seek spiritual help for wealth. It was supposed to be a simple, secretive task — selling spiritual items at 1 am. I said no. That decision changed everything in my life. Months later, I received a letter confirming I had won the United States Diversity Visa Lottery that I participated in the year before. When I heard this news of the lottery, many things ran through my mind. What if I had gone for that ritual and eventually died? What would have happened to my visa package? The answer is simple — it would have been a waste. Had I chosen that dark path, I might not be alive today.

That is the definition of someone dying before their glory. I pray we shall not die unfulfilled.

This experience taught me a critical truth: Every choice you make writes a line in your destiny story. Choosing patience and faith over shortcuts and fear shaped my future in ways I could never have imagined.

Success isn't an accident; it's a product of vision, patience, and persistence. From facing repeated university rejections to becoming the first in my family to earn a Master's degree in the United States. My journey is proof that *when preparation meets opportunity, favor is inevitable.*

There is a divine rhythm to life that only becomes audible when one awakens — spiritually and physically — to the reality of purpose. This awakening is not a gentle stir from sleep but a shaking of the soul, a piercing of the veil that once kept destiny hidden behind confusion, fear, and routine. When a person begins to awaken spiritually, they start seeing beyond the visible. They feel a pull toward something greater

It is more than just knowing you have a purpose. It's about feeling the fire inside, even when the world tries to drown it out. It's hearing that quiet voice at 2 am, telling you there's more for you than what your current reality shows.

Spiritual awakening is the moment your spirit becomes conscious of divine alignment. It is when the inner man becomes alert to the call of heaven that you realize that your existence is not a product of chance, but of intention. This awareness births clarity and conviction. Suddenly, what used to be acceptable becomes unbearable. Comfort zones feel like prisons. You begin to hear destiny calling your name in dreams, visions, and even in everyday conversations. Your discernment sharpens. Your hunger for meaning deepens. You recognize that there is more to life than survival—there is impact, purpose, and legacy.

This awakening penetrates the subconscious. The lies you've believed—"I am not enough," "I missed my chance," "I'm too broken"—begin to lose their power. Your thought patterns change. Your mind is no longer ruled by trauma, doubt, or generational patterns. Instead, you begin to think in alignment with what God says about you. This is the renewal of the mind that Paul spoke of in Romans 12:2.

While spiritual awakening is the ignition, physical awakening is the action. It is when your body, behavior, and decisions catch up with what your spirit now knows. You begin to move differently. You stop tolerating relationships, environments, and routines that contradict your calling. You start building, learning, stretching, sacrificing. You may begin waking up earlier, praying longer, speaking bolder, walking away from distractions—all because your physical life now mirrors your spiritual insight.

Your present starts to transform. Procrastination turns into pursuit. Confusion gives way to focus. This awakening affects everything—from the way you spend your time, to how you treat people, to how you speak to yourself.

Impact on the Subconscious

Once your spirit and body align, your subconscious becomes a garden for destiny. Seeds of greatness — planted by God and watered through pain, persistence, and revelation — begin to sprout. You no longer respond to life from a place of broken history but from a place of healed identity. Your inner voice changes. You start declaring what you used to doubt: *"I am called. I am chosen. I am rising."*

Effect on the Future

When destiny awakens in you, your future starts pulling you forward. You begin to sense divine appointments before they happen. The right people start finding you. Opportunities that once seemed out of reach begin to knock. Why? Because heaven responds to alignment. Destiny is not passive; it is a magnetic force that activates when you do. Your legacy begins to take form. Your children, your community, and even strangers begin to benefit from the overflow of your awakening.

Reflection Task

- **Ask yourself:** What has been stirring in my spirit that I've ignored in the physical?

- **Action step:** Identify one spiritual truth you've received lately. Write down one physical action you can take today that aligns with that truth.

- **Prayer focus:** "Lord, awaken every part of me — my spirit, my mind, my body — to the fullness of my destiny. Let my life be an echo of heaven's intention."

The Weeping Destiny

"When you allow the Holy Spirit to lead — not your fears, your timeline, or your preferences — you enter a flow where the supernatural becomes your normal. In that flow, destiny is no longer a mystery, but a path revealed step by step."

Chapter Two
The Irresistible Force

Destiny is mysterious. Sometimes it speaks in whispers, and other times, it screams through life's most intense moments. Your current condition is not your full story — it's just a paragraph in the larger book of your life.

There are spiritual forces — unseen but deeply active — that work behind the scenes of our lives. These forces are not random; they are intentional, divine currents that pull us toward purpose. They orchestrate supernatural alignments, connect us to people, places, and moments we never planned for but desperately needed. At first, we may not recognize their influence, but as life unfolds, we begin to see the thread of destiny they weave through every challenge, every delay, and every breakthrough. These invisible hands of providence shape our path, often quietly, yet with undeniable precision. They draw us into divine encounters that shift our trajectory and awaken our true assignment in life. When you learn to discern and yield to these forces, your life begins to align not just with goals — but with God's plan.

To walk in step with these unseen forces, one must cultivate spiritual sensitivity. This doesn't come by accident; it is developed through stillness, prayer, and a willingness to let go of control. Many people miss their divine alignments because they are too busy trying to force outcomes or interpret everything with logic. But destiny doesn't always follow reason — it follows revelation. The more you train your heart to listen, the more you will discern the subtle nudges of the Spirit. Sometimes it's a sudden unease that tells you not to take that job. Other times, it's a deep pull toward someone who ends up opening doors you didn't even know existed. When you allow the Holy Spirit to lead — not your fears, your timeline, or your preferences — you enter a flow where the supernatural becomes your normal. In that flow, destiny is no longer a mystery, but a path revealed step by step.

We often think destiny is something far away, a future event to look forward to. But destiny is happening now — in every choice, every "yes," and every "no." It's in the voices you choose to listen to and those you silence.

A striking and powerful example of divine orchestration is found in the life of Esther. She was an orphan, a Jewish girl living in exile, hidden in the shadows of a foreign kingdom. Yet, through a series of unlikely events — the dethroning of Queen Vashti, a nationwide search, and her selection as queen — Esther found herself in the very palace of the king. On the surface, it looked like beauty, timing, and coincidence. But in reality, God was positioning her for a purpose far greater than herself. When her people faced annihilation, it was Esther who stood in the gap, risking her life to intercede before the king. Her uncle Mordecai's words still echo through generations: *"Who knows if perhaps you were made queen for such a time as this?"* (Esther 4:14). She didn't get to the palace by chance — it was divine alignment. Even when God's name isn't explicitly mentioned in the book, His hand is evident in every detail. Esther's story shows us that when we yield to divine timing, even our hidden seasons can become platforms for destiny.

I remember seasons in my life when nothing made sense — when every door I knocked on seemed sealed shut, and every effort I made ended in silence. It was during one of those dry, confusing seasons that I began to sense something deeper at work. I didn't have the language for it then, but now I know: it was the pull of the supernatural — the hand of God redirecting my steps. The very moments that looked like delays were divine reroutes. The people who walked away made space for those who were destined to walk in. In hindsight, I see that destiny doesn't always come in loud announcements. Sometimes, it's in the quiet nudge, the strange restlessness, the sudden connection, or the unexplainable peace. These are the whispers of the unseen, aligning you with something greater than your plans — your divine purpose.

Your life today is the result of choices made yesterday—decisions acted upon or ignored. That's why it's essential to guard your influences. The wrong advice can derail a divine appointment, while the right choice can unlock blessings for generations.

In 2005, I finally accepted a cousin's persistent invitation to enter the American Diversity Visa Lottery. Before then, I had always refused. But that one time, with just 500 naira, I said yes. That decision changed everything. What if I had dismissed it again?

The stories of Joseph, Esther, and even my own life are not isolated accidents — they are threads in a divine tapestry woven by unseen hands. Destiny is not a straight road; it is a journey of faith, surrender, and divine timing. The supernatural realm is always at work, nudging, aligning, and preparing you for moments that matter. You may not always understand the delays, the detours, or the doors that refuse to open, but trust this: God is never idle. When you remain sensitive, obedient, and rooted in Him, He will position you in rooms you didn't campaign for and give you victories you never imagined. So don't just chase success — pursue alignment. Because when you are aligned with heaven, destiny will find you, even in the most unlikely places.

Take every little victory as they come. You should not take for granted small beginnings. Destiny doesn't always arrive with flashing lights or fanfare — it often comes disguised as a whisper, a gentle nudge, or a simple decision.

Many people hesitate because they fear failure. But failure is not the opposite of success — it is part of success. The courage to try despite the risk of failure is what separates those who fulfill their destiny from those who don't.

"Success is not final; failure is not fatal: It is the courage to continue that counts." — Winston Churchill

Let this chapter be your reminder: It's okay to fail. It's okay to fall. But what's not okay is refusing to rise.

Reflection:

Take a quiet moment today. Sit with God in stillness — no distractions, no requests, just openness. Ask Him:

"Lord, where are You trying to lead me that I have not discerned?"

Reflect on moments in your life that didn't go according to your plan, but somehow still led to growth, provision, or unexpected favor. What doors closed that ended up protecting you? What delays turned into blessings?

Task:

Write down three past events in your life that at the time felt like failure, rejection, or confusion — but now, in hindsight, you can see God's hand in them. Next, write down one area of your life today where you need to trust God's unseen hand. Pray over it, surrender it, and speak this declaration daily:

"I may not see the full picture, but I trust the One who is painting it. I am aligned with heaven, and my destiny will not be delayed."

The Weeping Destiny

"Self-talk is a spiritual discipline. It shapes your mind, emotions, and behaviors. Words create your reality. What you say to yourself when no one is watching becomes your truth."

Chapter Three
Positive Self-Talk

One of the greatest mistakes people make is waiting for external validation before believing in themselves. You don't need a prophet to tell you who you are—you are your own prophet. The words you speak over your life carry immense power—creative and transformational power.

Stop waiting for applause. Speak life into yourself.

You were not created to suffer or to lack. In the beginning, God created abundance—and He intended for you to enjoy it, and to dominate over everything He created.

In 2003, at just 23 years old, I wrote down my life goals: to marry before 30, to build a house before 35, and to make millions. Years later, I looked back at those declarations with tears in my eyes. I had entered the United States shortly before my 27th birthday. I married and became a father at 29, built my dream home at 39, and completed my master's degree at 40, and recently I received admission into a Doctorate (PhD) program. Why? Because I spoke life—and followed it with faith and action.

Self-talk is a spiritual discipline. It shapes your mind, emotions, and behaviors. Words create your reality. What you say to yourself when no one is watching becomes your truth.

- Tell yourself: I am not a failure.
- Remind yourself: I have a divine purpose.
- Declare daily: My background does not define my future.

If you don't speak life, the world will speak death into you. The enemy's goal is to mute your voice. Don't let him. Say it loud: *I will succeed.*

Positive self-talk is also about replacing negative, limiting beliefs with empowering ones. For example, instead of saying, *"I can't do this,"* say, *"I am learning, and every step brings me closer."*

You can reprogram your mind like a computer — overwrite the old destructive scripts with new, life-giving ones.

Death and life are in the power of the tongue, and those who love it will eat its fruit."
— Proverbs 18:21 (NKJV)

There are many students, professionals, and dreamers who fall short of their potential — not because they lack talent or intelligence, but because they are prisoners of fear. Fear of failure. Fear of not being enough. Fear of what others will think. And more dangerously, fear that speaks so loudly, it silences the voice of truth within them.

But to conquer fear and self-doubt, you must learn to speak life into your soul. Words are not just sounds — they are seeds. What you declare over yourself can either grow into confidence or grow into chains. The words you speak shape the world you experience.

That's why Scripture says, *"As a man thinks in his heart, so is he"* (Proverbs 23:7).

Don't second-guess your worth or calling. You are not an accident. You were fearfully and wonderfully made — crafted with purpose and intention by a God who doesn't make mistakes.

Instead of feeding your thoughts with worry, feed your spirit with the Word of God. Develop the habit of positive, faith-filled self-talk.

Tell yourself:

"I can do all things through Christ who strengthens me" (Philippians 4:13).

"The Lord is my light and my salvation — whom shall I fear?" (Psalm 27:1).

"I am more than a conqueror through Him who loves me" (Romans 8:37).

Confidence doesn't mean you'll never feel fear. It means you've decided to trust God more than you trust your doubts. It's not about having all the answers — it's about knowing the One who holds all the answers.

Let your inner voice echo the promises of heaven. Let it speak life, let it speak victory, let it speak purpose, and let it speak destiny. Be your own prophet.

Remember: If you constantly say, "I'm not enough," you are arguing against God's truth. But when you say, "I am chosen, I am equipped, I am victorious," you are coming into agreement with heaven — and heaven always wins.

Train your thoughts like a warrior. Ground yourself in Scripture. Cast down every lie and every fear that rises against the truth of God's Word (2 Corinthians 10:5). Feed your mind with what God says, not what fear says.

Every time doubt whispers, respond with this truth:

I am a child of God. I am not alone. I am walking on purpose. I will not fail.

Because the greatest battles are not fought in exam halls, boardrooms, or stages. They are fought — and won — in the mind and in the spirit.

Reflection Question:

What have you been saying to yourself lately — and does it align with what God says about you?

Prayer:

Lord, help me silence the voice of fear with the truth of Your Word. Teach me to speak life into every area of my heart. Let my thoughts and my words reflect the greatness You've placed within me. I declare that I am capable, I am chosen, and I am walking in divine purpose. In Jesus' name, Amen.

Practical exercise:

Start a daily journal where you write affirmations — statements that declare who you want to be and what you will achieve. Read these aloud every morning with conviction.

The Weeping Destiny

"Many people's destinies are dying — not because God failed them, but because they failed to wake up. The autopilot life is safe, but it's not satisfying. Be alert. Be intentional. Be present. Destiny doesn't work on cruise control."

Chapter Four
A Life on Autopilot

Many people are going through routines day after day without conscious awareness or purpose. They work hard, but their efforts lack direction. They exist but don't truly live. There's a silent danger that creeps into the life of even the most passionate believer — living on autopilot. You still wake up, dress well, attend church, go to work, interact with family, and check all the boxes of daily life. But inside, you are disengaged, numb, and disconnected from divine direction. You are moving... but without meaning.

Autopilot is not about laziness. In fact, some of the most hardworking people are often the ones stuck in it.

Many people aren't living; they're merely existing. That's not life. That's survival.

You were not born to be a robot, functioning on autopilot. You were born to thrive, to create, and to inspire. But when destiny cries and we don't respond, we gradually settle into patterns that limit us.

Years ago, I found myself going through the motions. I had a job, a family, and responsibilities—but deep down, I knew I wasn't fully alive. I prayed, but my heart was dry. I showed up, but my mind was elsewhere. That's when I realized: existing isn't enough. I had to break the cycle.

I was once trapped in this cycle. Exhausted and grinding endlessly, surviving on caffeine and painkillers, I thought pushing harder was the answer. But deep down, I was breaking down. What I really needed was stillness — rest for my body, mind, and spirit.

The Prodigal Son: Distraction Without Direction

Perhaps the clearest portrait of a life on autopilot is the prodigal son (Luke 15). Though he was a son by identity, he wandered away in pursuit of pleasure, affirmation, and independence. What began as freedom turned into famine. He ended up feeding pigs, spiritually bankrupt and emotionally lost.

Then something miraculous happened:

"And when he came to himself..." (Luke 15:17)

That's the moment the autopilot broke. He realized where he was, remembered where he came from, and made the decision to return. The father ran to meet him. Not with condemnation, but with compassion. That's what God does when your lost purpose finds its voice again.

David: Routine Without Accountability

David, the man after God's heart, also experienced the danger of spiritual disengagement. In 2 Samuel 11, during the season kings went to war, David stayed home. His routine became his ruin. With idle time and no spiritual accountability, he fell into adultery with Bathsheba and committed murder to cover it up.

He went on with life as if nothing happened — until God sent the prophet Nathan to confront him.

It was in that confrontation that David woke up. Psalm 51 is his soul's cry for revival:

"Create in me a clean heart, O God, and renew a right spirit within me."

David found redemption not through perfection but through repentance. Autopilot ends the moment you respond to correction with humility.

Peter: Passion Without Depth

Peter was bold, fiery, and full of declarations. He told Jesus he would die for Him, but when tested, he denied even knowing Him — not once, but three times.

He thought he was ready. He wasn't.

But after the resurrection, Jesus sought Peter out — not to shame him, but to restore him:

"Simon, son of John, do you love Me?"

Three times Jesus asked, and three times Peter answered. With each answer, Jesus reinstated him:

"Feed my sheep."

Peter went on to become a pillar of the early Church, preaching boldly and living with unwavering purpose. His revival began when grace met his guilt and called him into deeper commitment.

The Pattern of Revival

In each of these stories, we see a redemptive pattern:

1. Awareness – A moment of clarity awakens the soul.

2. Return – A step back toward God with humility.

3. Restoration – God never turns away a returning heart.

Autopilot gives the illusion of productivity but steals your potential. It causes you to miss divine appointments and opportunities for growth. You do the things that revive you – walk, play, pray, journal. You can call that friend who speaks life. Listen to the inner cry of your destiny. This requires intentionality.

Life on autopilot is safe but unfulfilling. Destiny demands your full presence.

The good news? Okay, hear it, you can switch gears. You can interrupt the pattern. You can choose to live intentionally.

Here's how:

- Reflect: Ask yourself hard questions. "Am I where I'm supposed to be?"

- Reset: Adjust your routine. Inject time for prayer, silence, creativity, and connection.

- Reignite: Reconnect with your passion. What once made you excited?

Don't let life pass you by. Reclaim your purpose. Wake up and live again.

Many people's destinies are dying — not because God failed them, but because they failed to wake up. The autopilot life is safe, but it's not satisfying. Be alert. Be intentional. Be present. Destiny doesn't work on cruise control.

Reflection Questions:

- Have I been living with routine but no revelation?

- What am I doing out of habit, not calling?

- Have I drifted from intimacy with God, while still performing spiritually?

- Is there a moment like Samson's, David's, Peter's, or the prodigal son's that I need to embrace?

The Wake-Up Call

Autopilot can feel safe. You don't have to feel. You don't have to take risks. But it also shuts down your destiny. The beauty of grace is that no matter how far you've drifted, no matter how long you've gone numb, God still knows how to awaken you.

"It is in the stillness after the storm that you begin to hear purpose calling through the noise."

So, pause, breathe, and reflect. Then act. Your life is not meant to drift — it is meant to drive purposefully, with clarity, intimacy, and boldness.

Let this be the chapter where your heart returns to the driver's seat.

"... sometimes, the most spiritual thing you can do is sit down and weep. Your tears speak where words fail. They are prayers wrapped in emotion."

Chapter Five

Rebuild

When the walls of life collapse around you, you have two choices: remain buried in the rubble or rise and rebuild. The process of rebuilding is painful—it demands honesty, courage, and sacrifice. But it's also liberating. It's where broken pieces become a new masterpiece.

You will fall. It's inevitable. But the real test is not how many times you fall, but whether you choose to rise again.

Consider Samson, a man of great strength and purpose who lost it all but was given a chance to rebuild. Unfortunately, he chose to surrender to despair instead. Don't make the same mistake.

Don't let failure write your final chapter. The greatest gift a person of destiny possesses is the ability to rebuild after collapse. You must be willing to start over, even from nothing.

After college, I struggled to find work. I walked past schools looking for teaching opportunities. One day, a school caught my eye with colorful flyers. I stepped inside uninvited and asked for a chance. They gave me one. That moment was a turning point. It showed me the power of persistence and faith.

After arriving in America, I faced more hardship than I ever imagined. The glamor I had seen in movies vanished in the face of cold nights, language barriers, cultural shock, and economic struggle. There were days I questioned why I ever left home. But deep within me, I knew I was here on assignment.

Rebuilding doesn't mean returning to what once was — it means creating something new from the ashes.

Sometimes, rebuilding your life requires starting from what looks like the bottom. And that's okay. Every strong building needs a solid foundation — and sometimes, old ones must be torn down for new ones to rise.

Your rebuilding may look different — a new job, forgiveness, a fresh start, or releasing toxic relationships. Destiny doesn't promise smooth roads but demands obedience, resilience, and faith.

Your due season is real, but only the obedient can access it.

Rebuilding doesn't happen overnight. But every intentional act becomes a brick in your new foundation. Keep laying them—one dream, one prayer, one step at a time.

No matter how broken your past is, your future can be whole. Start again. Rebuild, and this time, build it with purpose.

Don't give up just before your breakthrough. Start rebuilding with what you have. God multiplies faithfulness.

There are moments in life when everything you hold dear crumbles before your eyes. The job you thought was secure vanishes. The marriage you believed would last forever falls apart. The dreams you nurtured die silently in the shadows of disappointment. In those moments, it feels like destiny itself has wept over your story.

But loss is not the end. Failure is not final. Even ruins can be rebuilt. Your ruins are not your end. In God's hands, they are the blueprint for your restoration.

One of the most powerful biblical examples of restoration is found in the story of Nehemiah. He was not a prophet or a priest, but a cupbearer — a man with a burden. When he heard that Jerusalem, the city of his ancestors, lay in ruins with broken walls and burned gates, he didn't dismiss the news. He allowed himself to feel. *"When I heard these things, I sat down and wept..."* (Nehemiah 1:4).

Nehemiah wept, but he didn't stop there. He fasted, prayed, and sought God's direction. He took his pain to the only One who could turn ashes into beauty. That's the first step to rebuilding after loss: bring the broken pieces to God.

We live in a culture that often encourages us to move on quickly, to suppress our pain and fake strength. But genuine healing doesn't begin with pretending; it begins with presence — the presence of God in the midst of our wreckage. Nehemiah shows us that sometimes, the most spiritual thing you can do is sit down and weep. Your tears speak where words fail. They are prayers wrapped in emotion.

As he prayed, Nehemiah didn't only ask for help — he also took responsibility. He confessed the sins of his people and his father's house. Sometimes, before restoration comes, there must be repentance. Not all loss is caused by sin, but all healing requires humility. We cannot rebuild on the same broken foundations that once caused the fall. Healing may begin with pain, but rebuilding begins with honesty.

Then came the next step: action. Nehemiah approached the king with a request that could have cost him his life. But favor found him because he had first found God's presence. This teaches us that divine favor flows through divine alignment. When God is truly behind your rebuilding, doors open that you could never force.

When Nehemiah arrived in Jerusalem, he didn't start building immediately. He took time — three days in silence — to observe the damage. He went out at night to inspect the broken walls. Why? Because true restoration doesn't skip the hard part. You must see the ruins clearly before you can build correctly.

Have you taken time to inspect your ruins? Many people try to build again without addressing the pain, the patterns, or the pride that contributed to the fall. But a future built on denial is destined to collapse. Healing begins when we stop lying to ourselves.

Then, with resolve, Nehemiah stood before the people and declared: *"You see the trouble we are in... Come, let us rebuild the wall of Jerusalem, and we will no longer be in disgrace."* (Nehemiah 2:17). It wasn't just about bricks. It was about dignity, destiny, and restoration of identity.

But the moment he started rebuilding, opposition came. Sanballat and Tobiah — symbols of distraction, mockery, and fear — rose to discourage the work. They tried everything: ridicule, threats, and plots. Isn't that true for us too? The moment we begin again, everything seems to rise against us.

That's why Nehemiah's strategy is powerful: work with one hand, fight with the other. That is the posture of rebuilding. You build with faith, but you war against fear. You lay bricks with courage, but you guard your mind with prayer. Because the enemy doesn't just attack your progress; he attacks your focus.

In just 52 days, the walls were rebuilt. Fifty-two days after years of devastation. It wasn't just a construction project—it was a spiritual resurrection. Jerusalem stood again, and so did the hope of the people. This is what God does. He doesn't just patch up the damage. He resurrects purpose. He restores identity. He rebuilds better than before.

Reflection:

- What dreams in your life have collapsed like the walls of Jerusalem?

- What area of your heart still lies in ruins?

- Are you willing to allow God to walk through the rubble with you, gently revealing what must be removed and what can be redeemed?

Task:

Take a quiet moment today. Find a journal or piece of paper. Write down three areas of your life where you feel something has been broken or lost. For each, write a short prayer — an honest one. Not polished. Just raw. Then below each prayer, write one step you could take this week to begin rebuilding. A phone call. A conversation. A prayer. A fast. A declaration. One brick at a time.

Final Encouragement:

Destiny sometimes weeps, but it never dies. What breaks you, can also build you if placed in Divine hands. The God who called you is the God who will restore you. Your ruins are not your identity. They are the backdrop of a greater story — the story of a comeback, a resurrection, a rebuilt destiny.

Let the rebuilding begin.

"When God is preparing you for something greater, He will often allow things to slow down — not to punish you, but to process you."

Chapter Six

The Cry of Destiny

There's a moment in every person's life when the weight of purpose begins to stir restlessly in the soul, compelling you to pursue purpose with urgency. It doesn't always make sense. It doesn't always follow logic. But it's unmistakable. It's the moment when comfort becomes a cage, and you can no longer pretend that you're satisfied with survival.

You may not recognize it at first, but deep down, something begins to feel out of place. You sense there is more to your life than what you're currently living. That inner pull? That's destiny awakening—and it often shows up disguised as discomfort.

Most times, I pondered and self-reflect, I envisioned a life when I should have been happy—I had shelter, some income, health—but there was an aching hollowness inside. That void was purpose unfulfilled. I knew I was made for more, but I didn't know how to access it. That's the cry of destiny: it's the groaning of potential trapped inside complacency.

Destiny doesn't shout; it whispers in silence, nudges in stillness, and groans in dissatisfaction. It cries not because it's weak, but because it's waiting—for you to respond. Can you hear it? That silent, aching cry inside — the voice that wakes you up at night whispering, *"There's more."* That is the cry of your destiny. It is weeping.

Destiny weeps when you settle for less than your purpose. It weeps when you waste time chasing things that don't matter. It weeps when you silence your own voice.

At the altar of destiny, many are tempted to question God when the journey becomes painful or unclear. Yet in all of Scripture, only one destiny was designed to end in suffering and death—Jesus Christ. Though it was foretold that He would die for the sins of the world, even Jesus prayed earnestly for the burden to pass from Him. Still, He surrendered: In the book of Luke 22:42, Jesus said, *"Not my will, but Yours be done."* He was beaten, stripped naked in front of His mother, humiliated, and crucified—but through it all, He fulfilled the very purpose for which He was sent.

Contrast that with Samson—another man with a divine calling, a man that was lionized from birth. While his strength was legendary and his mission clear, his end was not God's intended outcome. Samson was not killed by his enemies; he chose to die with them. He asked God for vengeance, not redemption. He had a final chance to be restored, but instead he sought death. How tragic that one so anointed died defeated, when he could have lived to fulfill more.

Beloved, your destiny still breathes. Jeremiah 29:11 reminds us that God's plan is to give us a future and a hope—not destruction. You may have stumbled, strayed, or sinned, but if you're still alive, your purpose is not lost. The cry of your destiny is not for death or defeat—it's for redemption, restoration, and fulfillment. Hear that cry. Return to your purpose.

Don't let anything distract you from the glorious end God has planned for your life.

Destiny has a voice. It calls for hope, and if you listen carefully, you'll hear it in the still moments — begging you to rise, to fight, and to believe again.

Destiny doesn't beg forever. If ignored too long, it gets buried beneath distractions, addictions, busyness, and fear. But if you answer, everything changes.

Listen, destiny doesn't just require desire — it demands patience, timing, and divine alignment.

There was a period in my life when everything felt delayed. Nothing I prayed for came quickly. My plans were perfect on paper, but in reality, doors stayed shut. I wondered, *"God, where are you?"* But what I didn't know then was that divine delays are not denials. They are seasons of preparation.

When God is preparing you for something greater, He will often allow things to slow down — not to punish you, but to process you.

Think of Joseph. He was sold by his brothers, falsely accused by Potiphar's wife, and forgotten in prison. From the outside, it looked like his dream was dead. But every setback was a setup. The pit couldn't stop him. The prison couldn't contain him. Because destiny always prevails in God's time.

I remember meeting my wife years after we both unknowingly attended the same Holy Ghost service at The Redeemed Christian Church of God Camp ground, along Lagos-Ibadan Expressway in Nigeria. She had written the sermon title in her journal: *"Open Doors to Irreversible Blessings."* I was in that church program that night. Years later, we met in the United States of America, in a different country, and fell in love. Coincidence? No! That was destiny — calibrated and divine.

Nurture your destiny like a garden. Water it with discipline. Prune it with sacrifice. Protect it from weeds — negativity, distractions, and time-wasters.

There's a due season for your destiny — wait for it.

During my waiting season, I learned this: destiny is not just about where you're going; it's also about who you're becoming on the way there. God is not only taking you to the promise; He is making sure you're mature enough to handle it when you get there.

I had to grow. I had to heal. I had to learn how to steward blessings, not just chase them.

There was a time I lost a job I thought was my breakthrough. It was sudden and painful. But if I had stayed there, I would have missed the opportunity that led me into my true calling. It taught me never to hold too tightly to what looks like security — sometimes, God removes the good to make room for the best.

Timing is everything in destiny.

Rushing ahead of God will leave you frustrated. Lagging behind will cause you to miss key opportunities. But when you learn to move in rhythm with the Holy Spirit, doors open effortlessly, and peace becomes your compass.

Have you ever seen an eagle fly? It doesn't flap constantly like other birds. It soars by finding the right wind current and gliding on it. That's what walking in divine timing feels like. You don't force it—you flow with it.

There were moments I wanted to give up on writing, moments I questioned if anyone would even care to read my story. But then God reminded me: *You didn't write this just for you — this is someone else's survival guide.*

Destiny is not always about fame or fortune. It's about fulfilling the purpose for which you were born. And that purpose is always tied to serving others.

You may feel unseen right now, but heaven is watching. And when the time is right, nothing can stop what God has set in motion.

Let me encourage you: Don't rush your process. Don't despise the waiting. Use this season to prepare, to grow, to listen, and to align. Destiny is a journey, not a sprint. And if you stay the course, your due season will surely come.

So, rise each day with hope. Walk with expectancy. Speak life over your purpose. And trust the God who holds your times in His hands.

Your destiny is not behind you. It's ahead of you—right on time.

Destiny is not a luxury. It's a sacred responsibility.

When you give your destiny the attention it deserves, it returns fulfillment, peace, and legacy beyond measure.

When destiny cries, don't ignore it. Don't drown it with noise, or numb it with distractions. Lean in, listen, and let it guide you. Romans 8:22 says, "For we know that the whole creation has been groaning together in the pains of childbirth until now." That's not just about nature—it's about you, and about me. It is about all of us who know deep within that we're called to something higher, but feel the weight of delay, rejection, and fear.

The cry of destiny doesn't come to destroy you; it comes to awaken you.

It's what stirred Moses to leave the palace and identify with his people. It's what woke Esther from royal luxury to stand in the gap for her nation. It's what pushed Nehemiah to rebuild broken walls with trembling hands and a burdened heart.

You may not have all the answers. You may not feel qualified. But if you're willing, God can do more with your obedience than with someone else's experience.

Every groan is a signal. Every cry is a call. And every burden is a clue.

Answer the cry. Destiny is weeping… but not without hope. It's waiting on you.

Other Books by the Author

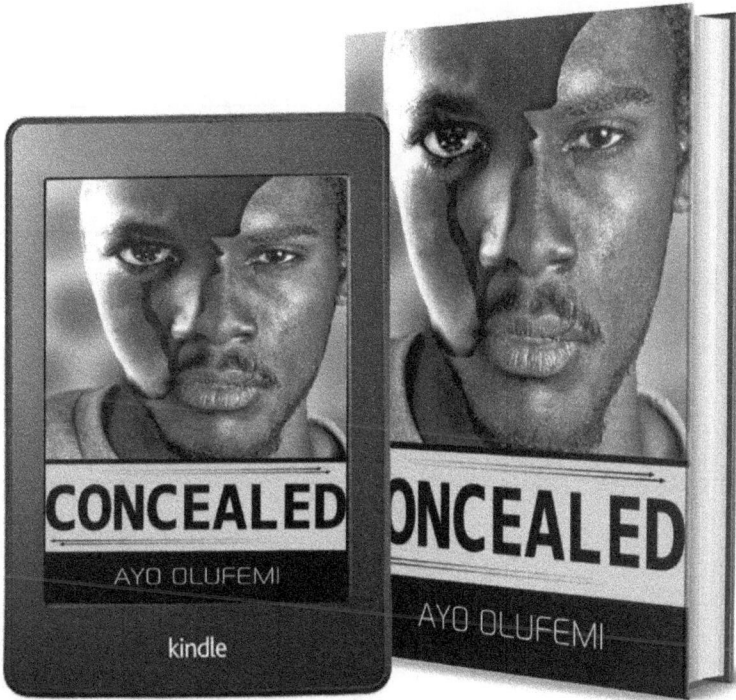

www.ingramcontent.com/pod-product-compliance
Lightning Source LLC
LaVergne TN
LVHW041206080426
835508LV00008B/825